T0063246

CRAZY LOVES CRAZY

LOSING FAITH

Neal Thompson

authorHOUSE®

AuthorHouse™ LLC
1663 Liberty Drive
Bloomington, IN 47403
www.authorhouse.com
Phone: 1-800-839-8640

Published by AuthorHouse 08/15/2014

ISBN: 978-1-4969-3377-5 (sc)
ISBN: 978-1-4969-3378-2 (e)

Library of Congress Control Number: 2014914529

THE STARS ALIGN

About Faith? That's a double meaning in many ways. Is she coming back? And that's why things are this way? Boy, I will try to explain Faith. The first part is my Faith, my Faith in knowing that my new start was going to bring her and, after 1-year there and 2-years by myself, we found each other; no bullshit. I can't figure out who found whom, but I had never fallen so fast in my life. She was perfect, perfectly broken.

It was early fall in Idaho the first time I laid on eyes on her. I saw her at the annual Demolition Derby with another man. I remember asking Brad, one of Kevin's greenhorn mechanics, "Who's that girl?"

"That's my sister," he replied.

"Is she hooked up with that guy?"

"I don't know," he answered, "I don't keep track of my sister."

Then Kevin pulled up in the car and started yelling and pointing at the engine of the car. I ran over and looked through the hood. One of the plug wires had come off. I reached slowly past the hot headers and reconnected the wire. Kevin revved the engine and gave me the thumbs up. I turned to let Kevin head back, and I saw her walking through the crowd of people. She turned, smiled at me, waved and kept walking with him. It would be weeks before I would see her again. It never occurred to me that she would change my life.

It was a busy morning at Kevin's Auto Shop. I had stopped by to talk to Kevin about some snowmobile parts. While we were talking in the parking lot, I saw her again.

"Wow you like her, don't you?" observed Kevin.

I turned to him and smiled. He yelled at Brad to come over and told him that Neal liked his sister.

Brad laughed, "Hold on let me talk to her."

He walked off and a few minutes later came back and handed me a piece of paper. On the paper was her name and phone number.

"What did she say about him?" Kevin asked.

"She said he's gorgeous."

We all laughed. I was so excited about having her number. I went to Kevin's office and hid. I was so nervous. I had her phone number!

Kevin followed me and asked me what I was doing.

"Hiding," I replied.

"Well she wants to talk to you so get your ass out there. I got up and walked out to the parking lot. She was waiting for me on the other side of the parking lot. She looked at me and asked me when I was going to call her.

"In a couple of days," I replied.

"Can I have that paper back?" she asked.

I took it out of my pocket. She grabbed it from me and started drawing a map on it.

"This is how you get to my house. You will pick me up at 6:00 tonight."

"Sure," I said.

She stood there looking at me; I reached over and took her in my arms in a quick hug. She felt good in my arms, like we had known each other forever. It felt right, she felt right.

"See you tonight," I said.

"Don't forget," she answered.

"I won't."

She got back in her car and drove away. I watched her until she was out of sight.

I went back into the shop and Kevin wanted to know what she said. I told him that she wanted me to pick her up that night.

"What did you tell her?" he asked.

"What do you think I said dumbass?" I answered.

"She is pretty young. Are you sure you're too old? She might hurt you," he joked.

"Yeah, but what a way to go." I stated.

I went home and got ready for my date. I was nervous and excited. It had been a long time since I had been out with a woman, and she was beautiful. Later that night I followed her map and found myself at her front door. I swallowed back my nerves and made my way up the steps.

When I knocked, her mom answered the door in a brightly colored, tropical printed mumu and said, "Come on in. Mary isn't ready yet."

My first impression when I entered the trailer was one of darkness and clutter. Her father was sitting on the couch watching a football game. I decided to be friendly and sat down and asked him who was playing.

He looked at me seriously with a hint of a sneer on his round face and said, "You'll have my daughter home by 11:00 and respect her virtue."

I was taken back and didn't know what to say.

"I had no other intention towards her," I stammered.

Mary came into the room and looked at me talking with her father. She said nothing and made her way out the door.

"Looks like we're going. I'll see you guys later," I said and followed her outside.

When I got to the truck, Mary was already sitting in the passenger side. I got in and started up the truck and as soon as I started to leave she turned to me and said, "I can't believe you were talking to me dad."

"Why? Shouldn't I talk to him?"

"He's a really mean man and had a gun next to him under the newspaper," she replied.

"That's ok. Mine is right here." I said and moved my shirt back to show her the gun I had holstered to my belt.

She smiled and snuggled closely up beside me. I was a little confused as to how fast things seemed to be progressing. Here it was 5 minutes into our first date and she was practically in my lap.

She asked me, "What do you want with me?"

All I could think was, Wow! Look at you absolutely beautiful, and that's what I told her.

She said, "I have a unibrow."

I said, "No you don't." And laughed.

"You have one too," Mary said.

We laughed all the way to the restaurant.

She smiled and nothing much was said until after dinner. The movie theater she said we were going to go to was closed; me being new in town, thought she should have known that. We talked, and she said we should go to the Falls.

"In the dark?" I asked.

"Yeah, it'll be fun," she responded, so off we went at nine o'clock at night.

She showed me how to get there. It was early fall, so it was somewhat cold when we got there. We had been kind of snuggling in the truck on the way there. She meant me at the back of the truck, and we were face to face in the moonlight. It was very romantic, so I kissed her, no tongue. She tasted like the strawberry gum she had been chewing. She was delicious.

The second time we kissed, it was deeper-passionate and intimate. I was spun, feeling her young breasts and firm body up against mine. All thoughts of going for a walk left my mind; I just wanted to hold her.

Out of respect for her, we walked in the dark for a while. I couldn't see anything, but I was holding her hand and following her. It felt like the trail was getting narrow, so I slowed her down, and we stopped there and held each other in the filtered moonlight and stars.

She looked me in the eyes and said, "I'm a virgin."

I was a little shocked and replied, "That's okay."

She began to cry and told me that the guy she was with had shown her porn. He tried to put her ankles behind her ears, but it wouldn't fit. I was stunned and couldn't say anything, so I just hugged her.

She had her arms around me as if we had known each other for a long time. When she was done crying, we kissed a little more and made our way back to the truck. It was getting late, around 11:00 or so. I told her I had better get her home.

We drove back towards her house. I parked trailers down from hers.

"Why are we stopping here?" she asked.

"I thought we could talk and kiss a little. You are already late." I wanted some privacy without her parents watching. We kissed, and I told her if her mom and dad were upset, they should blame it on me, when really it was all her. She was already calling the shots in this relationship.

When I dropped her off at her house, she asked, "When will I see you again?"

Trying to be a player, I answered, "Saturday." It was Thursday.

She didn't like that answer and asked me if I would pick her up Friday for lunch.

"Okay," I said and drove back to my house on the mountain.

All the way home I was not on this planet, I was surprised I didn't crash. When I got home, the dogs were happy to see me and seemed to smell her on me. I stood there in the quiet house awestruck of Mary. Her smell was all over me, and I wanted to see her again. Neal was in love.

The next day after very little sleep, I was up early cleaning the house, thinking of her. I found myself counting the minutes until noon when I would see her again. I picked her up at the trailer for lunch like we agreed. This time she came out to the truck and we left.

She asked me, "What are we going to do?"

I told her that I had a lot of work at home to finish on my truck. She seemed very excited to see my place, and I was very excited to show it to her.

Knowing the women I have had in my life over the years, I didn't want to tempt this one with money or fame. All she knew was I had a house, an old Toyota pickup and two Pomeranians. I thought of the old empty cabin on the road below me, and decided I would take her there first.

We pulled up to the old cabin and she said, "That's your house? Well you did say you've been working on it. I guess it'll do, I'll help you." And out of truck she jumped to go nest.

I started laughing and told her to come back to the truck. She came back and asked me if I was laughing at her.

"You're funny. That's not my house," I said.

"Really?" she replied.

"Get in," I answered.

We drover further up the mountain and pulled into my real place. The look on her face was priceless. We went inside, and the princess was home.

She looked the house over carefully and, after a minute or two said, "It's very nice."

"Thank you," I replied.

"So what are we going to do now?" she wondered.

"Winters coming," I replied, "and I have a lot of work to finish on my truck."

She replied, "Okay. Can I help?"

"Are you sure? It's dirty work," I stated.

"I don't mind." She assured me.

So off to the shop we went. We both spent some time sanding on the truck. Eventually, she asked me how she was doing. When I went to check her progress, I was surprised to see that she had sanded down to the bare metal, which was about 2 layers farther than I wanted to go. I couldn't bring myself to tell her that though- Shit, what motivation! Instead, I told her she was doing a great job and suggested that she move her sanding over a bit.

After a while, out of nowhere, she asked me, "Do you smoke marijuana?"

My first thought was, "who calls it that anymore?" Before I could voice an answer, she asked me if I had any.

I smiled and responded, "That stuffs illegal," and went back to sanding.

She looked upset at my response but went back to sanding the pickup anyway.

"Hey Mary?" I said. She looked at me, "Do you want smoke some weed?"

She smiled and jumped down from the truck. We headed back into the house and burned one, and the ride started. She was so funny when she was high. We worked and laughed through the evening.

"I think I should take you home now Mary."

"Not yet. Let's have dinner and watch a movie," Mary answered.

"Dinner sounds awesome," I replied, and I was right, it was awesome.

She made spaghetti, a salad, and bread. Watching her in the kitchen made my heart skip a few beats. She was so young and beautiful. It had been a long time since a woman had cooked for me.

"Dinners ready," she said.

I sat down and, had almost taken a bite when she stopped me, our eyes met. "We have to pray first."

I found myself thinking, "I've found the perfect woman."

"Sure honey. Let's pray," I said aloud. We held hands while she blessed the meal and us.

After dinner and a movie, it was almost 1:00 a.m., and I told Mary we needed to get her home. I didn't want her parents so worry. She argued with me saying she didn't want to go home and wanted to stay with me. I pointed out to her that I didn't even have a phone for her to call home with. I left her in the house and went out to warm up the truck. I found myself waiting for a bit and still no Mary. I went back inside and called to her from the kitchen.

I heard her respond, "Come here." She was in my bedroom.

When I walked into the bedroom, I saw that she was in my bed. I asked her what she was doing and told her she needed to go home. Her response was to pull the blankets aside. She was completely and beautifully naked.

"Come here. I want to stay with you".

I paused for a second and asked, "Do you know what you're doing?"

Mary answered, "Yes, I love you."

Keep in my mind that as honorable a man as I am, I was also awfully lonely and had been without a woman for a couple of years by then. It didn't take me long to join her naked in bed.

We touched and stroked each other for a long time. I had never felt like this before. We talked a bit, and she told me she wanted me to have her virginity but was scared.

"It's a big bed. Just go to sleep," I responded. She was scared and I didn't want her to feel like she had to.

"No," she said.

"Are you sure?"

"Yes," she said, "right now tonight."

I touched her in every sensual way I could think of, I kissed her from her ears to her toes, lingering in some places a little longer than others. She was squirming from my touch and begging me, "Please, please, don't hurt me.""Are you really a virgin? "Yes. Nothing not even a finger well once

I put an icecube in it." How did that go? "It was really cold and it would not come back out". We both laughed.

She seemed to have decided that missionary would be the position. I was 36, she was 21, I was thinking of carburetors to control myself. I found myself looking into her eyes, as I slid gently inside of her. I was amazed how good she felt. Carburetors were fleeing fast from my mind. She felt incredible wrapped around me. She was moaning under me and biting my shoulder, and I couldn't hold back any longer. I pulled back at the last minute, as much as I wanted to stay buried inside her, I didn't think we needed a baby. I lay down on her warm body, and we held each other for a long while.

"I love you," she said."

"I love you too. Are you okay?"

She assured me she was feeling good and was more than ready to go again. I chuckled, "Give me five minutes." We spent the rest of the night making love, discovering Mary's newfound sexuality. She liked more than just missionary.

Morning came, and I found myself in disbelief. I couldn't believe this beautiful woman was really in my arms.

When she woke up, she looked into my eyes for a few seconds and said very softly, "I love you."

I gripped her a little tighter and said, "I love you too." It had been a long time since I had said that to any woman, but saying it to Mary felt right.

"Wanna go again?" she asked coyly.

I was on top of the world.

Later that morning, we left to go to the mud bog, and stopped at a local café to get a bite to eat. I asked her to please call her parents; she did. When she returned from the phone call, she told me, "Everything is fine." I could tell that wasn't true. I paid the bill and tip and went to gas up the pickup. She stayed in the truck while I went in and paid.

Walking back to the truck, I noticed that Mary was crying uncontrollably in the seat. I hurried to the truck and saw her Dad pulled up on the other side of the gas pump. He was out of his car and in my face instantaneously. My first thought was that he wouldn't try anything physical; I was younger than he was and most of my stress was worked off on the weight-bench- I was right. He was yelling at me that I had sex with his daughter, and I needed to marry her. I explained to him that it had been a late night, and I didn't have a phone for her to use. I did have two bedrooms though, and she had spent the night in the spare room, I assured him nothing had happened (He didn't believe me). I told him that this wasn't the time or the place for this conversation, and I would bring Mary home after the mudbog. He wasn't happy, but I walked away from us and got in the truck. Mary was still crying. We left.

"Everything will be fine," I told her, and we all know what fine means. She seemed to know right then and there that her family would be the end to our love. Her father's intimidation and control was something she couldn't escape. If I had known then what was to come, I would have listened to her and we would have run away. But I didn't, and the worst was yet to come.

We had a great time at the mudbog. I introduced her to a lot of my friends. Most of them were surprised to learn she was Brad's sister; he was a geek and she was gorgeous.

After the mudbug, I took her home. On the way to the trailer, she told me she didn't want to go home.

"We need to talk to your parents"

When we pulled up, we saw that all of her stuff was on the porch. She found a note left with her belongings that read, "Mary you're 21. You're on your own. Good luck. - Lynda (her mom) and Richard (her dad). Mary was dumbfounded. She showed me the note and started crying. I tried to reassure her, telling her I loved her and we'd figure this out, and she could stay with me.

I got out to help, I couldn't help but notice that her belongings fit in 4 hefty bags. I helped her load the garbage bags and her bike, and we went home to our house.

THE NEXT 12 DAYS

The next 12 days and days after will be hard for me to explain, but I'll try. She was the perfect insta-wife. I worked; she cooked and cleaned. We worked on the truck together and almost finished it too. One day, while she was in the shower, I did a little snooping and looked through her purse, but there was nothing to see- no money, no credit cards, or even any makeup, just a learner's permit.

When she got out of the shower, I asked her if she had a driver's license.

"No," she replied.

"Why not?"

"They wouldn't let me," was her reply. I assumed she meant her parents.

A day or two later, after more bite marks and rug burns on my knees, I started noticing other things. One night after dinner, I held up my flashlight and asked her what it said. It was quiet. I looked at her, and she was quiet again. She couldn't read!!! Where I grew up I didn't think this stuff still happened, but I loved her, and she said she loved me, and I wanted to help her.

For the rest of our 12 days together we did just that. We filled our days with anything that I thought would help her, driving lessons, reading lessons, shopping together. We talked about her family's problems with us, and I had told her to leave her mom and dad alone- they would come around.

A week after she moved in with me, I had driven her to work. We were sitting in the truck making-out before she had to go in, when I opened my eyes to her mom's face stuck to the window.

"Mary, your moms here."

She turned around and rolled the window down and her mon said "Hi guys. We are really sorry everything started off the wrong way."

Mary responded telling her mom she was happy and starting a new life. Her mom said they were sorry again, and we talked a little. Lynda invited us over for dinner. I told her that would be great, and Mary and I would discuss it and call them. Mary kissed me hard, opened the door pushing her mom out of the way and went to work. I went back home to pass the time until I would see her again.

Later, when I went back to pick her up from work, she seemed upset. I asked her what was wrong. She told me that her parents had asked her to come over for dinner on her break and, when she had, they told her they wanted her to come home.

"What do you want to do?" I asked her.

"I want to stay with you, "she said.

"Well ok then," I replied.

That night at home, she asked about my day i told her i worked on the truck for a while then went down the mountain to see my other girlfriend; as a joke; she hit me in the face really hard. I was laughing she was not; poking me in chest saying you are my Neal don't you forget that! I won't. She chased me out of the house and into yard, and tackled me from behind, after wrestling for a few minutes we went back in the house. She was still acting weird, so I suggested that she sit down and talk to me. We talked, and she told me she wanted to run away with me, get married and build a house in the woods. (Normally this would have been too fast for me; I've never been married, but with her it felt right.)

I replied, "I'll marry you Mary, but we already have a house in the woods."

"I want to go away, where no one can find us," was her answer. I reassured her, telling her we would be fine here.

That night we watched Man on Fire. We lit some candles and had a fire burning. As I sat there with her head in my lap stroking her hair, she asked me (pointing at the TV), "Would you do that for me?" Our eyes met, and I said, "Anything for you."

After the movie, we went to bed. She had the room all set. It was very romantic, and my heart was racing again. After days of this, I was beginning to worry about my abilities. We talked and just held each other at first.

"Boy, I created a monster," I teased her.

"Grrr," she replied playfully and climbed on top of me. I felt like I was 21 again.

Later that night, she woke me to ask me why I did that?

I rubbed my eyes and asked, "Did what?"

"Why don't you stay in me?"

I wanted to tell her, "Baby, I would like to stay in you forever." But what I said out loud was, "You don't want to get pregnant."

She told me she would like to have our baby, and I said not until we are older and you have finished school.

"You're going too fast Mary, slow down," I said gently.

She told me she loved me, and I told her I could see that, "I love you too."

When I picked her up from work the next evening, she came out with flowers for me and seemed happy. We talked about her day.

"I'm glowing. Everybody at work's been asking me, and I told them about you, and I love you and you love me."

On the way home, we stopped at the grocery store and picked up some stuff she needed. Boy! Women need a lot of stuff, but I was happy not to be bachelor-shopping and being in public with a hot young lady made me feel good! She drove home; she was really getting the hang of driving a stick. When she did miss a gear or a corner, we both laughed but inside I was also a little scared-about more than driving. Was this moving too fast? Would her parents always be a problem? What would the future hold for us?

After dinner that evening, we talked about her- actually, she talked and I listened. She told me about her awful family life and how cruel her dad could be. How they wouldn't let her drive or go to school. (The way I saw it, she was 21-years-old but had never had the chance to be like most young women).

I told her we would finish getting her a driver's license and a car and then work on getting her GED. After that, we would get her into college. I would pay for it and maybe some professional counseling.

"You think I need a shrink?" she demanded.

"Maybe- You are telling me some very dark problems here and they may take a professional to help you with."

"I think you're right," she said.

We made love that night and again in the morning. That girl was the energizer bunny when it came to sex. She asked if you can make love in the shower. "Sure you can, well let's try it!!" In the shower with hot soapy water running over us, she asked how we are going to do this. Ruff ruff Mary. She laughed and took her position, I put my arms around her from behind and started massaging her large firm breasts while biting her ear and kissing her neck. She arched her back and pushed and I was deep in her again! It was a good thing I was in shape or I wouldn't have been able to keep up.

We were early again the next day when I took her to work, so we spent some time kissing and holding each other before she went in.

"I'm going to be late for work"

"Go," I said, "I'll see you tonight."

She got out of the truck, and I watched her intently, as she walked away- everything about her was incredible.

She walked around the front of the truck, stopped, turned, and said, "I love you. What do you want for dinner?"

"I love you too Mary. We'll figure dinner out later."

She smiled at me and walked away.

COMING UNGLUED

I went back later to pick her up, but she never came out. I fell asleep in the truck, with Huggy and Bee (my two dogs). When I woke-up, it was late, 11:30 p.m. I started the truck and drove around to the front of the hospital to the emergency room entrance. I walked inside, and the fat lady behind the glass was giving me the evil eye. I asked her if Mary was still working and told her I was here to pick her up. She snarled back at me that Mary had left with her parents a long time ago. This bitch wanted to fight, but not today. I left and went home. I spent the night confused, wondering where she was and what was going on. Was she ok? Did her parents have her? Would I see her again? The thought that she didn't want me anymore ran through my mind.

The next day I went to visit my friend at his shop (where Mary's brother worked). Both of them were wondering where I had been. I told them I fell asleep behind the hospital and went home. I just figured she didn't want to see me anymore. They told me they had been looking for me all night.

"Mary was kidnapped by her parents, and Richard's got a gun and says he's going to kill you."

"I thought she didn't want me anymore," I replied.

"No," Kevin answered, "She loves ya man. We have to help her."

"What can we do?" I asked.

"Go to the cops. Her dad is probably beating her as we speak. He's got her locked in the trailer," Kevin responded.

I loved her and she obviously needed my help. I took my gun off my ankle, placed it Kevin's desk, and headed to the sheriff's office.

After a while, an officer came out and asked what the problem was. I explained that my girlfriend hadn't come home, and her brother had told me some weird stuff about her mom and dad. I told him I was worried about her.

"Can you help?" I asked.

The officer told me that they would do a drive-by welfare check.

"Great," I responded.

He wanted to know had to get a hold of me and, since I didn't have a phone, I told him I would come back tomorrow and check in.

I went back to Kevin's shop and got my gun, and he and I talked for a bit. Then I drove home. My mind was reeling with thoughts of whether or not she loved me, or really needed my help, or had she just dumped me?

The next day I went back to Kevin's shop; it seemed to have become the headquarters for the "Let's Help Mary" campaign. We decided to see what the cops had found out the day before. Once again, I left my gun in the desk (if you carry legally, you still can't take a gun in a cop shop, courthouse or bar).

When I got to the police station, it was the same as before- hurry up and wait. Then it started getting weird because the same cop came out, this time with four or five of his buddies with him. He told me to follow I did, and they led me to a storage room at the end of the hall.

"What did you find out?" I asked.

They started circling me, I was wondering what was going on.

"Put your hands on the file cabinet and don't move," they ordered.

I did, and the cop behind me started patting me down. When he was finished, the older cop had them check my ankle again and asked where my gun was.

"You shouldn't take a firearm into a police station," I answered.

They all looked puzzled by my response. Then they asked me where all my drugs were.

"We're going to search your house anyway."

"I only have a little bit of weed. I'll tell you where it is if you don't trash my house. I have a nice house and nice stuff," I said.

They agreed, and I told them where to find the weed at my house. They led me outside to the parking lot and put me into the back of the police car. I watched as they searched my truck but didn't find anything. The older cop came over to me, acting as if he was my buddy, and asked what kind of shotgun I had. I answered his question and asked him if I was under arrest?

"No. We're detaining you for our safety and yours," was his answer.

"Well good then," I said, "Could you take the cuffs off then?"

"Doesn't work like that," he retorted. "What kind of shotgun do you have and why is it by your front door?"

I told him the type of gun I had and explained that there was a bear getting into my garbage. The gun was to scare it away. We left with a caravan of cops and NARCO cops.

When we arrived at my house, the cops were already searching my property and outbuildings with a dog. After an hour or so, they took me to the front of the house and asked where the weed was.

"We got your pipe."

"I told you where it was." I said.

"Show us."

We walked into the shop, and I pointed to my old desk. They found my stash. After more searching, I think they started to feel stupid for making such a big production out of a little bud. For a couple of minutes, it was just guys BSing in the shop. Two of the cops really liked my truck and made lots of compliments on my camouflage paint job and tires but then back to business.

"We're taking you down to the station until we verify what that is."

"What about my dogs? You have them locked in an old car."

The older cop told me not to worry. It would take 30 minutes. They just wanted to verify what the drug was and would write me a ticket.

When we got to the station, they put me in a holding cell. After what I figured was two to three hours, I started pounding on the door. Finally, the jailer showed up and opened the door.

"What?"

I told him I needed to piss right now and wanted to use the phone.

"No one let you do that?"

I told him no, and he apologized for them losing me during shift change. I called Kevin.

He told me that they had been looking for me.

"I'm in jail jackass. Get me out now!"

"What! Are you kidding?" Kevin asked, "Why?"

I explained to him what had happened, and he told me he would be there in 10-minutes. He arrived with Brad and paid my $100.00 bail. Kevin seemed to think the situation was funny, but I wasn't laughing.

Kevin, Brad, and I headed outside. Suddenly, Brad took off running, jumped into Kevin's truck, and squealed away right in front of the cops. I couldn't figure out what he was doing. Then I saw Richard. He was across the street in the grocery store parking lot, yelling at the cops for letting me out of jail. Brad skidded the truck to a stop beside his dad. He jumped out of the truck and started yelling. His Dad started yelling back, and fists and feet started flying. A police officer headed over, and Kevin and I moved closer. I saw Mary in the parking lot by the van crying. Kevin asked the cop why he wasn't doing anything but, by that time; Richard and Brad were back to yelling at each other and not fighting anymore.

"Come here Mary. I love you," I yelled to her. She didn't answer me and only cried harder.

Richard noticed Mary and I, ran over, grabbed her by the hair, and pulled her off her feet to the back of the van. He opened the door, bent her over using her hair, and, kicking her in the thigh, kicked her into the van.

At this point, Kevin was yelling at the cop, asking him to do something. The cop told us to shut up and sit down. He then slowly walked the rest of the way to the van. Richard had just started pulling away when the cop yelled at him to stop. The cop took Mary out of the van and talked with her for a few minutes. Then she got back in the van and left with Richard.

The cop came back over to Kevin, Brad and I, and explained that there was nothing he could do. Kevin protested and the yelling was on again. I didn't say anything because someone was about to go back to jail. Luckily, Kevin shut up and we left.

Back at Kevin's shop (it had now become Help Mary Headquarters), my confusion mounted. So many things had happened in such a short amount of time and not normal things either. The first thing all of us decided was that we needed information- who/what/where/when and why? Kevin and I geared up with scanners, VHF radios, a tape recorder, and guns.

I had been thinking of private investigating as a second career and had learned a lot about it before I moved to Bonners. I had decided that it would be a lot harder and more dangerous in the country, and I was right. It didn't take long for us to start the puzzle. The second attack came at Kevin in the form of slander. The cops and some church elders were telling people that Kevin was a major drug player in the drug world and that was where his money had come from. In reality, I had just loaned him $30,000.00 to buy a new house. The gossip told us that the parts store was the start of it, in particular, one cop and Jason, the storeowner's son. Therefore, I decided to investigate. Kevin and I rolled into the parts store in my truck. Jason was outside and, after some car bullshitting; I confronted him with what we knew. He wouldn't tell us who the cop was; just that he was a city cop and confessed the rest. I told him eventually he would have to spill it and, if he did it now, Kevin and I would try to keep him out of it. He told us. We showed him the tape recorder; the look on his face was priceless. By now, I knew that recording someone without his or her knowledge is legal in Idaho. Kevin and I left and went to discuss what we knew and what we had learned. We had stirred the hornet's nest.

The next morning, after another sleepless night, Kevin and I were drinking coffee and talking about Mary. He was convinced we would be able to get her back. I wasn't so confident. The scanner had been pretty quiet that morning. That is until it came across the scanner they were coming to the shop for me. I wanted to run, but Kevin reminded me that I had not done anything wrong. I waited and a few minutes later two sheriff's cars pulled into the parking lot at the shop. They walked into the shop and smiled at us. We returned their smiles and asked them what was up.

I noticed one of them had a lot of papers in his hand; his gun hand was free. We all had one close too. After a bit of a stare down, they asked me if I would go unlock my house or if they should just kick in the door. I asked them why, but I didn't get a response. I told them I would meet them there in 20-minutes. They left.

I asked Kevin to go with me to the house. On the way to the house, we were both confused. What did the cops want? It suddenly dawned on me, DNA! Kevin didn't think so, but I was convinced that was what they wanted. There wasn't any weed in the house anymore, but I had been so wrapped up in everything that had been going on that I hadn't had time to clean.

When we got to the house, the cops were waiting for me. All four of us went into the house, and I was right. They started digging in my drains and collected pubic hairs. I could hear them talking, saying that is his, hers are blond. They carefully packaged my clothing and bed sheets and took pictures of the inside of my house. I told them to take a picture of the roses Mary had given me; they did.

One of the policemen took Kevin outside and asked him, "Did he have sex with her?"

Kevin responded, "I'm a religious man. How dare you ask me such a thing?" The cop eased off.

Kevin asked a question of his own, "Why are you doing this to my friend? He moves here and brings his own money. He doesn't work, so you automatically label him."

The cop responded that this was a criminal rape investigation.

I replied, "No this is the tracks for your railroading me to prison."

The cops face turned red and he told me to shut up.

They asked about the shotgun I had by my bed. I told them that if anyone threatened their life, they would sleep with one too.

"Good point," the cop agreed.

"You've been a cop a long time, right?"

"Twenty-five years," he responded.

"Well after 25-years, I'm sure you know where the bullshit lies and you know I am not lying to you."

"I just collect the evidence" was his response, "I don't make the decisions." With that, they both left.

Kevin and I went back to the shop. Kevin wanted to strategize, but I wasn't in the mood and went home.

My mind was racing. In less than 2-weeks, I had fallen in love, had mind-blowing sex, been

27

to jail and was looking at prison time; the worst of it all was Mary was gone, and my Mary was fading fast. I sat in front of the fire, in the dark and alone; I started to cry and looked at my 45 pistol. I thought that pulling the trigger might be better than prison. Then there was a knock at my door. I didn't feel much like company, so I didn't answer it. Then Aron, Kevin's younger brother, pushed open the door.

He came over and sat down by the fire with me. "Neal, it's going to be okay."

"I don't think so man," I replied, and tears streamed down my face. He asked me to give him the gun, I didn't. I did, however, put it down on the floor. Then Kevin and Mary's brother Brad came into the house. They all tried to be positive, telling me that they knew I hadn't raped Mary. All of us knew that if Mary got on the stand and pointed her finger at me then I would be going away for a long time.

Kevin offered to let me stay at his place for a while. He didn't think I should be alone, "At least until things cool down," he said.

"I don't want to impose on your family man," I responded.

"It's okay bro. I love you," Kevin retorted.

I wouldn't have been able to get to the house without you. So we made Kevin's house base camp.

The next day, we all talked- Kevin, Allen, Brad and I. They all knew, as I did, that the fight was on or I was going to prison. What could we do though? Brad said maybe if I go over to the trailer park, I could get her away from Mom and Dad. I believed she would come with me. Kevin came up with idea of calling in a noise complaint to the police, so they would investigate, and Brad could show up and try to talk to Mary.

"Let's do it," I agreed.

That night, at 1:00 a.m., Plan-A went into action. Brad and I drove towards town, carefully doing the speed limit. We monitored our scanners and radios. I parked in a dark back alley, and we waited for the call to go over the scanner as planned. When we heard the call, Brad got out of the truck and headed to the trailer. All I could do was wait.

A half-hour passed, and still no Brad. The radios were quiet by this time. I thought about leaving, hell I wanted to leave, but I couldn't just leave Brad there. We had decided no radios at night because they use the same VHF scanner that the cops used. We could hear them, but they could also hear us. We assumed that our cell phones were bugged. Finally, Brad came back to the truck.

"Well, what happened," I asked.

"Nothing. There were no cops. Nothing. I pounded on the door and ran and still nothing," he explained.

"Let's get out of here. Something isn't right," I said.

Back at Kevin's, we spent the night talking and planning. Brad told us a lot about his family. He told us about the abuse they all suffered, not just from Dad but from Mom too. She was also a hitter.

I suggested to Brad that maybe we should call his older sister and see if she could help. He agreed it was worth a try.

The next day Brad called his sister, Debie. Kevin talked with her and explained the situation. She had already been told one side of the story but said she didn't believe it. Mary was a fighter, and the story didn't make much sense to her. She said she believed us and wanted to help Mary and I. She told us how she had planned to marry her boyfriend, but her mother and father had forbid it and locked her in her in her room. She ran away in the middle of the night with her friends and escaped to Montana. She had married her boyfriend the following morning before her parents could stop her.

Kevin asked Debie to speak with police and try to help Mary. She said she would and told us she would call us back. She called us back with disturbing news. The cops wouldn't tell her anything, just that there was a huge investigation going on, and she should stay out of it. I thought to myself, "Investigating the wrong man."

Debie told us that her Dad would take Mary to his family in Northern California and have her committed; we would never see her again. Kevin and I left the room to discuss everything that had transpired. Everything was getting crazier by the minute.

"What do you think we should do Neal?" he asked, "I'm a drug-dealer and you're a drug-dealing rapist."

"I think the only way to help me, is by helping Mary. All they have on you is rumors," was my answer.

It was quiet for a few minutes, and then Kevin said, "We'll get her back bro, I saw her with you, and I know she loves you."

"We have to bro," I replied. "She is the one." I started to cry.

That night I went back to my house. I wanted to make sure everything was okay and be alone. I needed to think and process this entire messed-up situation. I made a fire and sat down. The dogs were happy to be home, but they seemed to know something was terribly wrong. I had stashed some weed in the backyard, where no one could find it, and went and got it. I sat in front of the fire and smoked a little, but it didn't help. My life was on the line. My brain had shifted into high gear, and there was no slowing it down. By 4:00 am I thought, "What am I doing here?" I needed to be closer to Mary.

I put my boots back on and drove to my neighbor John's house. I pounded on the door and woke him and his girlfriend up. He wanted to know what was going on, and I told him, "I need your help. My girlfriend has been kidnapped by her psycho dad, and I think he is going to kill her."

"Give me a minute to get dressed. I'll be right out," he hollered.

He came out and got in the truck.

"Now calm down and tell me what you're thinking," he said.

"I need to be closer to her. I can't just sit home and do nothing. Her dad is a nut job, and I'm scared for us both."

"I'm with you buddy," he agreed. "What do you want to do?"

I replied, "Let's go to the hospital and wait. Its close enough we can watch the trailer but far enough away that I won't get in trouble with the restraining order. But it's close enough we can see what's happening."

It didn't take long before John noticed we were being watched. Minutes later the van was speeding away. I tried to follow but was cut off by a logging truck. By the time we got going again, we had lost them.

"What now?" John asked.

"I think he is taking her to Cali," I replied.

"Are you sure?"

"No, but it's all I have to go with," I grimly replied. Her sister had said that's what he would do.

"We don't have enough money to get to Cali," John remarked.

I pulled out the $5,000.00 I had.

"If you get caught with that they're going to think you're a drug dealer and take it. Give me half to hold, and we'll be cool," john suggested. I did.

By now, we were already 15 miles towards California, breaking all the speed limits. After a while, we still couldn't find the van, so I stopped in another small town and asked the cops for help. They made some calls and said it wasn't their problem. John and I left and kept heading for Cali. We stopped in Washington at John's brother's house and left my gun with him. Even with a concealed weapons permit, I knew California wouldn't be cool with it. We followed the Columbia River to the Oregon coast. The truck had started to vibrate in a bad way miles ago, and John and I decided we had better stop and check it out.

At the next gas station, John removed the front driveline, and I filled both tanks of the truck with gas. We left, and the vibration was gone. When we got to the California border it was late, and I had been driving since 6:00 am, so we stopped at a motel for the night. We had a much-needed cocktail and food. I called Kevin and explained where I was and what we were doing.

"I just saw the van here in town. You're losing it buddy," he said.

"Huh," I replied. "Be home in the morning."

The next day, at the shop, Kevin and I talked about the next step and decided that Richard's van needed to break. It needed to appear not to be sabotage. Am old mechanic had told me about putting mothballs in the gas tank; it makes it run great for a bit and then the heat will melt it down. That night, Kevin and I parked a few blocks away with his girlfriend Becky. Kevin volunteered to do the mothballs, so I wouldn't get in more trouble than I already was in. He quietly left the truck and headed towards the van. Becky and I waited.

"Neal, this is some crazy shit. I'm sorry it's happening to you."

"Sometimes a man only has two choices- stand and fight or run, and I am not running yet."

"I wish Kevin would hurry and get back," Becky said, "seems like he's been gone a long time."

"Yeah, he has been, but he has his radio. He'll page twice if something goes wrong, and we'll get out of here," I replied.

Then I saw Kevin staying in the shadows, making his way back to us. He got in and said, "Bro I wish you had been there. It was so quiet; you could hear the mothballs falling into the tank."

"I hope it works," I said. He started the truck, and we left.

The next morning, when I woke up at the house I made some coffee and looked out the window. I remembered a movie I had seen a long time ago and decided to go outside and turn my American flag upside down; It was a sign of distress. Then I went over to my truck and mounted an American flag on my truck. I grabbed a can of spray paint and wrote I Love Mary across the tailgate. I started the truck and headed to the shop. I made sure when I parked it was where everyone could see it.

When I walked into the shop, Kevin said Allen had seen the van in town.

"It might take some miles to work." I explained.

"What are you thinking now?" Kevin asked.

I thought if I could just get her alone for a couple of minutes, I bet she would go with me. We could get married, and be on our honeymoon before anyone even realized she was gone.

"How are you going to get her alone?" Kevin asked.

"Halloween is tonight. I'll go trick-or-treating in costume. Maybe Mary will be handing out the candy. If she is, I'll lift my mask and say 'Let's go Mary.'"

"What if Richard is there?" he asked.

"Then I'll just walk away."

He agreed that it might work, and I headed to the store to get a costume, with plans to meet up later that night with Kevin. Later, with my Power Ranger costume, Becky and the kids were getting ready to go trick-or-treating. The kids wanted to know what I was going as. I showed them my costume, and Becky laughed, "You're really going to wear that?" she asked.

"Well I'm going to try. They didn't really have my size. Everything was sold out."

"Go and put it on then, so we can see," she laughed.

I came out of the bathroom with my costume on; it was not at all flattering to an adult male. Everyone, including me, laughed their asses off.

Becky laughed and said, "Lowell you need to tape that thing or something you can't go out like that."

"Why?" I laughed, "Is it too tight?"

"Well I hope it doesn't rip," Kevin added.

"Can you see my gun?" I joked. Everyone laughed.

"You are so going by yourself looking like that," Kevin said.

"Fine. Just make sure your radio is on." We left.

I had decided to hide my truck, so the cops didn't see it. I picked the place behind the parts store and the laundry mat. It was 2-3 blocks away and had no streetlights. Wearing a power ranger's costume, and carrying an orange plastic pumpkin with a flashlight and radio inside it, I headed towards her house.

There were a lot of kids running around trick-or-treating. I saw lots of cops driving around. One went slowly past me as I walked, but I kept going. I decided not to stop walking and loop around behind in the alley. As soon as I got in the alley behind the house, someone (I think Richard) jumped out from behind the bushes and lit up the alley with a spot light. I had a mask on, and the light was hitting me from behind, so I kept walking. Someone yelled, "Hey! Come here!" I just kept walking around the corner and out of the alley. I thought to myself, "the truck is 3-blocks away, just walk slowly, act like a parent watching their kids and get out of there."

By the time I got back to the truck, the suspicious activity call was already going across the scanner. I assumed it was probably because of me. Driving very cautiously, I went home.

That night, I sat and talked to the dogs. It had been almost a month since all of the craziness had started, but it felt like she had just been there yesterday. I found myself wondering why she didn't just stop all this. Her dad had probably told her that he would kill me and her, and she probably believed him. Poor Mary being torn in two directions. Hell, poor me. During another night of combat sleep, I had an idea.

The next morning I decided to hire an attorney. All the local attorneys I tried refused to take the case. They believed she was the one pressing charges; I tried to explain that it wasn't her, it was her dad. I couldn't get help locally. I decided to try a "big city lawyer", and drove to Coeur d'Alene. I had no better luck there, no one would help. I was on my own.

So I returned to the only people who would help. Kevin asked me how the trick-or-treating idea had worked out. I told him what had happened with Richard hiding in the bushes with the spotlight. Allen was there with us in the office that morning. He suggested that we just take Richard out.

"Yeah like they wouldn't be coming for me first," I said.

My idea was to fight crazy with crazy. Instead of taking out Richard, what if he took me out? If Richard were in jail, where he needed to be, then the pressure would be off Mary. She would recant her statement to the police.

Kevin asked, "So you're going to get Richard to kill you?"

"No. Not kill me but hurt me bad," I replied.

However, Richard was not going to be the one to do it. I would get someone else to do it. We would just make the cops believe he did it.

"Shit Neal. That's just crazy enough to work," Kevin exclaimed.

"Fight crazy with crazy bro, and I just showed for the fight."

I explained to Allen and Kevin how we would stage it. Hillbilly John would hit me because the

37

cops didn't associate him with us yet. He would be the one to tell the cops that he saw Richard hit me. Richard had already told half the town that he was going to kill me.]

"When are we doing this?" Kevin asked.

"Tonight the cops are going to charge me with rape any day now, and the plan won't work with me in jail. Are you guys gonna help me?"

"Sure Neal," they said.

"Good. Then I will go talk to John and meet you all back here at 8:00 tonight."

I found John at the lumberyard. I told him I needed his help and asked him to meet up with me at Kevin's shop later that night. Later that night, after all the players had assembled, I explained to John the plan. He said he didn't like it. He didn't want to hit me. I told him he would be saving my ass in the end and I needed him to do it. Kevin pointed out that Richard was a pussy and wouldn't take me on without a weapon, and we all agreed.

"What kind of weapon should we use?" I asked. Allen suggested a bat.

"No," I said, "a 2x4 is less deadly and harder to get prints off."

"Yeah, we can get one from the lumber yard, where he works," Kevin added.

Kevin suggested we take the customer's van out of the shop and use it. Allen went to get the van, and we all got in and headed to the lumber yard. No one was talking much. I was amped about doing something. As we drove around behind the warehouse, Kevin killed the lights on the van.

"Where are you going?" I asked Kevin.

"Chill, I worked here when I was kid. I know where I'm going," he answered.

The van finally stopped, and I got out and spotted a pile of scrap 2x4s. I grabbed one that looked to be about 4-feet long and was the width of a bat. We were back on the highway in minutes.

I handed John some latex gloves and told him to put them on. He was still trying to talk us out of it. I told him to stick to the plan and to wipe off the wood. I had forgotten to put gloves on.

The closer the van got to town, the more we kept rehashing the plan. Kevin stopped the van about a block away and said, "All right John, get out."

"Don't let me down dude," I said.

"I won't," he said and disappeared into the dark.

Kevin dropped me off at my truck.

Allen was so stoked; he was laughing as he said, "See you in the store Neal."

"Good luck brother; I love you," said Kevin.

I looked at the two of them and said, "Thanks for trying to help Mary and me. I hope this works."

Allen retorted, "Neal you got balls."

"All for love buddy." I smiled at them and headed to my truck.

My mind was racing with thoughts of Mary, trying to organize everything that had happened in such a short time. My heart was breaking; deep down I had a feeling that I would never see her again. I hoped I could keep myself out of prison.

I pulled into the store and parked. I decided to park close but off to the side of the store, right under the street light. I got out and headed into the store. To make it look right I had to buy groceries. After I shopped for few minutes; I saw Allen at the other end of the store.

"Shit, here we go," I thought to myself.

I wrapped up my shopping and headed to the registers to check out. Allen was at another register buying groceries, as we had planned. I left just a few minutes before Allen.

On the way to my truck, I saw John hiding by the corner of the store. I gave him a slight nod and kept walking. I put my key in the door to unlock it but couldn't help but look out my peripheral vision. John was just a few feet away. He swung.

He hit me in the back of the head just like we had planned. I saw stars, but I knew I wasn't going down. I heard the 2x4 hit the ground, so I launched my bag of groceries and fell back onto the ground in the dark and the rain.

I laid there in the rain hurting but not dead. After what seemed liked forever, I heard someone coming out of the store: it wasn't Allen though. The person knelt down next to me and asked if I could hear him. I mumbled a response. Then I heard Allen.

"Who hit me?" I asked weakly.

I pretended to be knocked out, figured the less I do or say the better. Within a couple of minutes, people from the store were gathering around looking at me. I could hear Allen telling everyone he had seen who did it. Then I heard the sirens coming. I started crying. It wasn't from the pain in my head but for Mary.

An EMT woman was talking to me, asking me question to see how coherent I was. All I would say was my head hurt, what happened, and where are my dogs? A lady from the store asked me what dogs I was talking about. I hesitated and said my little dogs in my truck. She said there weren't any dogs in there. I let the tears flow harder. She told me not to worry about anything. They would find my dogs.

I was loaded into the ambulance and taken to the hospital. I let my mind go and went to a happier place- Days before when I was so in love with Mary and planning a future with her; Praying before meals and making love like I had never felt before in my life.

At the hospital, they checked my vitals and asked questions about what had happened. I kept asking about my dogs. The nurse told me they were looking for them but hadn't found them yet. I knew the dogs were safe at home, but John hadn't hit me as hard as I was hoping, so I played it up a bit. It didn't take long before the cops showed up and started asking questions. I mumbled that Richard said he was going to kill me. At that point, the ER doctor told the cop to leave the room.

I was thinking to myself that I was hurt but not too badly. I had to be careful because overplaying it would blow it. Cop radios were going off in the doorway. From what I could hear they were looking for Richard. It was hard not to smile. My crazy scheme might have worked, and I might just see Mary again. The thought of that made me cry again. The nurses were trying to console me, but they were tears of joy not pain. The doctor asked me how I was doing. I told him my head hurt.

He smiled and said, "I bet it does. Do you remember what happened?"

"Not really. I saw someone, and then something hit me."

"It looks like someone hit you with a 2x4," the doctor replied.

"It feels like it too," I muttered.

"It sounds like it was your girlfriend's dad. What an asshole," he said.

I stared blankly at him and nodded in agreement. He explained that the police were going to come in and take some pictures of my head, and then he would be back to talk to me. I nodded. When I was getting a CT-scan done, one of the cops came in and began questioning me. He wanted to know if I remembered what happened.

"I know it might be hard after being hit in the head to remember but anything can help. Are you sure you didn't see who did this?" he asked.

"No," I said, thinking to myself that if Allen was playing his part right, I shouldn't have to be the one to point the finger.

"Have you been drinking tonight?" he asked.

"No," I answered.

The nurse gave him a look like "that's enough."

He took a few more notes and said, "Hang in there. Everybody's looking for the guy." Then he left the room. I just nodded.

Back in the ER, the doctor returned and said, "Well I don't think you're going to die. I think we should keep an eye on you for 24-hours."

"No," I replied, "I don't have any insurance. This is already pretty spendy I bet.. If you think I'm doing okay, I'll go home."

"I can't make you stay," he replied.

"Thanks for the help," I said.

"It's my job. But if you don't mind, what does the tattoo on your arm say? Hold on, let me read it."

"You can't without a mirror," I answered but, to my amazement, he was able to read it. He asked me if I had written it and I told him I had gotten it from a book. He went on to tell me how a few weeks ago his wife had gone to visit her sister; he had told her he was going to get a Harley and a tattoo while she was gone. He didn't get the bike but showed me the tattoo. It was a sun tattoo, with his kids' names around it. We shared a few laughs over his wife's reaction to it, and he wished me luck.

"Come back if you have any nausea or dizziness," he instructed.

"Okay Doc, thanks for the help."

A few minutes later the nurse came in and said, "I hear that you want to go home."

"Yeah, I can't afford to stay."

She explained that she couldn't let me leave by myself and asked me who she should call to pick me up.

"Call Kevin, I don't have anyone else," I told her.

She took down his name and phone number and left to make the call. She returned a few minutes later to tell me that she had gotten a hold of Kevin and although he had been sleeping, he said he would be there as soon as he could.

"Are you sure you will be okay at home by yourself?"

"Yeah I have some friends to help me," I replied.

"I'll come back and get you when your friend gets here."

About a half-an-hour later, Kevin came back with the nurse and said, "Bro are you okay? They told me to bring you some clothes. What the hell is going on?"

I answered, "I think Richard wacked me."

"Are the cops doing anything?" he asked.

"I don't know. Could you just get me out of here?"

"Okay. The truck is parked in the ER lane. Put some clothes on, and we will go," he replied.

The nurse wheeled me outside in a wheelchair and helped me get in. Kevin started it up and, and we drove away.

A couple of blocks from the hospital, Kevin said, "Bro that was the craziest thing I have ever seen. Forty-minutes after I left you, the scanner went nuts. Every cop around, even Idaho State and Montana, are looking for Richard! How's your head?"

"The lump?" I asked.

"Yeah, I already know about the other part," he answered.

"Fuck you," I replied, and we laughed a little. I joked, "Don't you know you can't hurt a Norwegian by hitting him in the head."

"I still can't believe you went through with it," Kevin exclaimed.

"All for love, Bro all for love," I responded.

"Well it worked; they are going to fry that fucking asshole. How come you don't look happy?" Kevin asked.

"I still have a bad feeling bro that she is gone, and I am never going to see her again.," I answered.

"Ah, come one man. You have to have a little Mary," he laughed, "Get it?"

"That's not even funny," I retorted.

"Yeah, it is. Don't worry Bro, we will get her back. I saw her with you. I know she loves you," Kevin came back with.

The tears started to flow again and I told Kevin to "Drive. Stop at the mini mart. I lost my Copenhagen."

One block from the store something caught Kevin's eye. It was Cole. He was walking half in the highway and crying.

"Fuck," Kevin said. "I forgot to tell you. Cole is messed up. He thinks he killed you."

"Well, let me out. You go tell him I'm fine and tell him to keep his mouth shut," I demanded.

When I got out of the store, Kevin told me that Cole was drunk and crying. He had told him I was okay, but he was still upset. He hadn't wanted to hit me in the first place.

"I hope he keeps his mouth shut," I said. Kevin agreed.

We drove to my house, and I thanked Kevin for driving me home. He decided to stay for the night. I tried to talk him out of it, but he insisted. We sat around the kitchen table in silence. It was eerie. The dogs were even quiet; no barkfest from either dog.

"Even the dogs are freaked out," Kevin observed.

"Yeah, they miss her too," I agreed, "she used to say they were our kids and make them mini-pancakes in the morning. I need to be alone Kevin, just take off."

"You sure?" he asked.

"Yes," I said. He told me to leave my radio on, so he could get a hold of me and asked me what I was going to do now.

"Be by myself for a few days," I told him.

"Call me in the morning," he replied and left.

The next day my radio squawked, "Oh brother where art thou?" That was our call sign.

I picked it up and said, "I don't know."

"I need to see you," Kevin replied, which was our code for don't talk on the radio. He told me to meet him at the clubhouse, another code for his shop.

I got to the shop, and I found Kevin in his office. He told me that he had bad news. Richard was in town, and it didn't appear that the cops were doing anything.

"They're saying you were drunk," he added.

"Fuck it," I said, "what about going to the newspaper. I'll give them the real story."

"Badass. Do you know where it is?" Kevin asked, and I shook my head no.

"Just down from the hardware store. Same side of the street," he continued.

"Alright," I said, "wish me luck."

As I was leaving Gary, Kevin's Dad, showed up. He had heard someone had hit me. I told him that a psycho dad had done it.

"They are saying I was just drunk though, so I'm going to go to the paper," I explained.

Gary replied, "I tell you boys right now the last guy that fucked with the cops was found crashed into the storefront with a bullet in his head."

"Who cares," I replied, "look at it this way, the woman I've been waiting for is gone. The chance I'm going to prison for something I didn't do is very high. Do you know what happens to Cho Mos and rapist in prison? I'll take my chances with the bullet."

Kevin chimed in, "Gotta do something."

Gary replied, "You're both fucking idiots."

"Whatever," I replied and left.

I found the newspaper office and parked the truck. It was hard to hide a camouflage truck in the city, so I didn't even try. I knew small town life, and the cops would know where I was within five minutes; all I could think about was what Gary had just warned- and Mary, I was always thinking about her.

Inside the newspaper office, a lady asked me how she could help me. I I told her that I had been told that they were doing a story on the assault that had occurred at the grocery store.

"I'm the guy, and I would like to tell the real story," I answered her.

She told me to have a seat while she went to speak with the editor. Shortly thereafter, she returned and led me down a narrow hallway cluttered with books and old papers. She rapped on the door jam. In the midst of cigarette smoke and the junk, a man appeared. He looked like he had been in that office longer than I had been alive. He moved some papers and boxes and found a chair.

"Sit down," he said, "tell me what you have to tell me. I don't have all day.

I sat down and started from the beginning. I could see he was taking notes When I was finished telling him my story, he said, "that's quite a story."

Back at the shop, Kevin asked me how it had gone and I recounted my trip.

The next day the paper came out and Holy Shit!, second page with pictures and a huge article that told most of the story. I took some hits for smoking weed, but the main goal of my concern for Mary was there.

Later that day, Brad got off the phone. He had been talking to his sister, Debie. They had his Dad downtown for a polygraph test.

Kevin smiled, looked at me and said, "Told you, you crazy son of a bitch. Now they will know Richard is a liar and lock him up."

I was speechless. It had been over a month since everything started, and holding Mary again had become a distant dream. I felt like if I were lucky, I would see her in my sleep. Then the phone rang. It was the cops. They wanted to interview Brad.

One the way to the Cop Shop, Kevin, Brad and I talked. They were both excited until I mentioned that if they were giving Richard a polygraph and asked him if he hit me, when he said "No", it would show he was telling the truth.

Kevin wasn't worried, "Dude they will just rephrase the question. Like, did you want to kill Neal, and the machine will blow up."

We dropped Brad off and told him to call when he was done. Kevin and I went back to the shop. He was counting his chickens, but I knew better. He could tell something was wrong with me and asked me what was bothering me.

"It doesn't feel right. It sounds too good." I explained to him,

"Come on cheer up. By tomorrow, you guys will be gone. Just promise me you will name one of your boys after me," Kevin said.

The phone rang, and it was Brad; they were done interviewing him. We went and picked him up. He told us how it went, and it sounded like the cops we relearning more truth than lies.

Brad said at the end of the interview, the lead narcotics officer had taken him aside and said, "We know now Neal did not hurt your sister."

Hearing that they finally believed me was too much, I started crying and was completely embarrassed. Kevin tried to reassure me, saying that he understood how I felt. The thought that I wasn't going to be going to prison kept running through my head. The n another thought occurred to me, and it scared me to death.

"Where is your sister? Where's Mary?" I asked Brad.

"I asked them. They said they were sorry but nobody knows where she is right now. And Richard won't tell them," he replied.

Kevin cut in with, "I told you Bro, now they will lock up that crazy son-of-bitch.

I could barely speak, and quietly asked again, "Where's Mary?"

"Chill Bro," Kevin inserted, "We are making progress. You will find her."

Kevin pulled into the shop, and we went into the office. Huggy and Bees had been locked in there while we were gone. I picked them up and headed for the door. Kevin stopped me and asked me where I was going.

"Home!"

I walked out and loaded the dogs into the truck.

"Hey!" Kevin called before I pulled out. "I don't have to worry about you do I?"

"No," I yelled at him. "We have been over this. Later."

We pulled into the driveway and parked. It was a crisp twenty-degree November afternoon. We went into the house, and it was thirty-degrees and empty. The dogs didn't even seem to be happy to be home. They were missing their little pancakes. I started a fire and sat down. Huggy jumped onto my lap and curled up. I gave him a few pats on the head. He turned and looked at me. I knew what he wanted.

"Sorry little buddy."

The fire was starting to warm the house up, and I felt helpless. I had no more ideas, good ones or bad. Out loud I said to myself, "I lost Mary."

I thought of how many things that really meant and laughed and cried all at once. It started getting dark, and the batteries that powered the house were dead. I got up and walked to the kitchen. On the table were a bunch of candles. I lit a couple, and I stood there watching the flames flicker.

The words "Sorry son, we don't know where your sister is" kept running through my head. Then I came to a conclusion that tore me into pieces. Mary is dead! The fucker killed her! It's over! All I could think was I spent twelve-days with an angel and God needed her more than I did.

At that moment I stepped into a place. I was terrified. Everywhere I looked I saw her. I could feel her in the room. I had let her down. I looked at my .45; it was calling my name, Without Mary, I wondered how I would go on. I picked the gun up and admired its beauty, how it glistened in the candlelight. My life started playing backwards in my head, and a voice inside told me Mary was in Heaven. If I pulled the trigger, I knew I would never see her again. Crying and laughing at the same time, I yelled, "Fuck" and looked up. I laid the gun on the floor and asked God to forgive me for not protecting his angel. Huggy and Bees came over, and Bees started spinning her circles. Her way of telling me she needs something. I got up and checked their bowls, they were empty. I filled them up and, while the dogs were eating, I figured my next move. The decision was instinctive- Gotta Go. But where?

I started throwing stuff into bags and crossed my fingers that the old Dodge Motorhome, also known as Dog Van, would start. I grabbed my hat, coat and a flashlight and opened the door. It was snowing; I knew that if it built-up, Dog Van wouldn't be going anywhere.

I made it out back and inside Dog Van. The lights came on, I took that as a good sign. I sat down in the driver's seat and noticed it was snowing harder.

"Please Baby," I said as I inserted the key, "Don't fail me know."

I nailed the gas four or five times and hit the key. Please crank I found myself begging, she coughed and died.

"Come on you old piece of shit, bitch, fuck and turned it again. She cranked slower, so I stopped and waited a few minutes. Huggy and Bees had already taken their spots on the passenger seats. I tried again, and she started!

"That's my girl," I thought to myself, "Now get me and these dogs out of here."

I realized the tarp was still on, so I got out and cut the ties. I couldn't pull the tarp off though; there was too much snow on it already. Fine, wanna play? I took all four ties ropes and wrapped them around a tree a few feet in front and got back in, found reverse and floored it. Dog Van flew backwards and ripped the tarp off! I pulled in front of the house and started loading. When Dog Van was loaded, the real fun was ahead-driving down the hill in the snow 'til we make it to the county road. Luck was with me that night though, it was more snow than ice and we made it to the highway.

I decided to stop and Kevin's on the way out. When I pulled up in Dog Van, he came out and wanted to know why I was driving such a piece of shit in the snow.

"The highway is clear, and I'm leaving this crazy town..."

"Why?"

"Haven't you figured it out? She's dead. Richard killed her!" I exclaimed.

"Calm down bro, you don't know that for sure," he replied.

"Yes I do. I can feel it! I felt it days ago man! I am never going to see her again! She's gone!" I yelled.

Kevin tried to calm me down, "Let's go in and talk."

"Fuck you," I retorted, "I'm done talking, I just stopped to say thank you and goodbye. Give this to the cops when you see them."

"What's it about?" he asked.

"Read it," I answered,

"Will you call me tomorrow? Let me know where you are?" Kevin asked.

"Sure," I promised.

Later, back on the highway, the snow was falling. It was late, and I sighed to myself. I was almost to the state line, and I couldn't wait to put some miles between us and the Vortex of Evil. I passed a sign labeled Rest Area Ahead, looked at the radio and saw that it was 3;12 am. I decided I should stop. When I slowed down to pull in, the dogs woke up. I turned off the highway. It seemed like all the truckers had the same idea. I found a spot in-between some long-haulers. I let the dogs out, and I stretched my legs while Huggy Bear and Bees ran around barking and peeing on everything that didn't run away.

I went back inside Dog Van and turned the heat up. I sat down with some beers and watched the snow pile up. I was feeling useless, wondering how long before the pain would stop. How long before I stop missing her? I decided that I didn't want the pain to stop, and I definitely didn't want to stop thinking about her. I picked up another beer and a pen and some paper. I drew my heart. I looked at what I had drawn- it was perfect. I needed to make it to the coast to the tattoo shop and have her put it on my left arm, so I could keep Mary close to my heart.

What do you do when you get to a place where everything you say sounds so crazy and people treat you different? I love Mary. Why is that so tough? What is Love? Where does it stop? If you are a man, a warrior, what do you do for the woman you love? Is your life whole without her? She is the one! If the Earth opens between you, would you not spend the rest of your life trying to cross the gap to be with her? She wanted my help so badly, and I could do nothing but die for her. That would kill the one goal, which is to see her again.

As much as I try to explain those twelve-days with Mary, it will always sound crazy. It was unbelievable. Call her retarded, call her naïve-She was untainted by the World. Crazy attracts crazy. Nobody's listening again.

Printed in the United States
By Bookmasters